Jokes and Riddles

(Originally titled *Jokes and Riddles to Read Aloud*)

Compiled by OSCAR WEIGLE

Illustrated by JESSICA ZEMSKY

and JOYCE BIEGELEISEN

GROSSET & DUNLAP
PUBLISHERS • NEW YORK

ISBN: 0-448-11884-X
© 1962, by Wonder Books, Inc.

CONTENTS

RIDDLE ME THIS

What is too much for one, just right for two, but nothing at all for three?
A secret.

What fruit is on a dime?
A date.

Where does Friday come before Thursday?
In the dictionary.

Why should bowling alleys be quiet?
So that one can hear a pin drop!

Why isn't it safe to keep a clock at the top of the stairs?
It might run down and strike one.

Why is the letter D like a wedding ring?
Because we could not have wed without it.

Why is it wrong to whisper?
Because it is not aloud.

Why is the letter D like a sailor?
Because it follows the sea (C).

What is the hardest thing about learning to ride a bicycle?
The ground!

What pine has the longest and the sharpest needles?
The porcupine!

When is a farmer cruel to his corn?
At harvest time, when he must pull its ears.

What animal has the head of a cat, the tail of a cat, the ways of a cat, and yet isn't a cat?
A kitten.

What pets make sweet music?
Trum-pets!

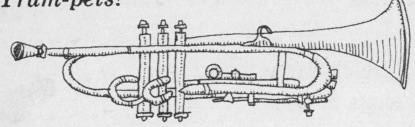

What is ferris?
A big wheel at the amusement park.

What animals are in banks?
Doe and Bucks.

What is the best thing out?
A fire!

Why is the sun like a good loaf of bread?
Because it's light when it rises!

What is the coldest row in a theater?
Z row (zero).

What is the best thing to put into cakes?
Your teeth!

Why is an empty purse always the same?
Because there is never any change in it.

What kind of cans may be found on the floor of the United States Congress?
Republicans.

What is more useful after it's broken?
An egg.

What has five eyes and goes south?
The Mississippi River.

How do we know that a dentist is unhappy?
Because he looks down in the mouth.

Why don't we ever have a minute to ourselves?
Because the minutes aren't hours.

What's the use of a snow shovel?
Snow use.

What can always be found between here and there?
"And."

What kind of a house weighs the least?
A lighthouse.

Why is a baby the least important member of a family?
Because it doesn't count.

When is a store like a boat?
When it has sales.

When are the roads unpleasant?
When they are crossroads.

What makes you sick if you take away the first letter?
Music.

What ring is best for a telephone?
Answering.

When is a child not a child?
When it is abed.

Why aren't baseball players going to use bats any longer?
Because the bats are long enough now.

What did the big chimney say to the little chimney?
"You're not big enough to smoke."

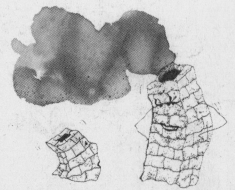

Why is a star like a window in the roof?
Because it's a skylight.

What is the difference between a postage stamp and a woman?
One is a mail fee and the other is a female.

Why would a spider make a good ball player?
Because it is good at catching flies.

What is the laziest mountain in the world?
Mount Everest.

If a carrot and a cabbage ran a race, which would win?
The cabbage, because it's a head.

How do you make a slow horse fast?
Stop feeding him.

Why should you never try to sweep out a room?

Because it's too big a job. Just sweep out the dirt and leave the room there.

What bird helps us eat?
The swallow.

What swimmer could jump in the water and not get his hair wet?
A bald-headed man.

Where should a dressmaker build her house?
On the outskirts of the city.

What kind of dog has no tail?
A hot dog.

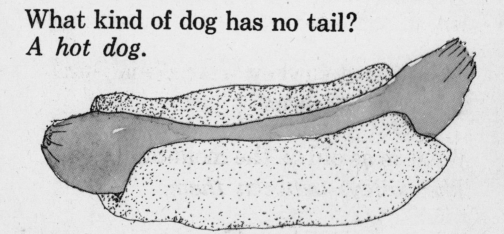

Why does a poor man drink coffee?
Because he has no proper tea.

Why do children have to go to school?
Because school will not come to them.

What is that which everyone can divide, but no one can see where it is divided?
Water.

What always has an eye open, but never sees?
A needle.

What do you call a man who is always wiring for money?
An electrician.

Why does a cowboy wear a wide hat?
To cover his head.

What is as old as the mountains?
The valleys between them.

Why is a dog that rides in an automobile like a covering for the floor?
It is a car pet.

Why is a ball team like a pancake?
Because its success depends on the batter.

A lady in a lunchroom was eating ham and eggs when a man came in and ordered coffee and pie a la mode. How did she know he was a sailor?

Because he was wearing a sailor's uniform.

What gets wetter, the more it dries?
A towel.

What word is pronounced wrong by even he best of scholars?
Wrong.

Why does an Indian wear feathers?
To keep his wigwam.

What wheel goes around without touching the ground?
A Ferris wheel.

What tree do people look for when they're hungry?
The pantry.

On what toe does a corn never grow?
The mistletoe.

Why shouldn't one trust the ocean completely?
There's something fishy about it.

When are boys like bears?
When they go barefoot.

On which side does a leopard have the most spots?
On the outside.

Why is your hand like a hardware store?
Because it carries nails.

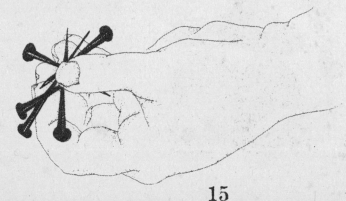

Who can raise things without lifting them?
A farmer.

If the king sits on gold, who sits on silver?
The Lone Ranger.

Why do snowflakes dance about?
They are getting ready for the snowball.

What is put on the table, cut, but never
eaten?
A deck of playing cards.

What is it that dances in the yard after it
is dead?
A fallen leaf.

What is bought by the yard but worn by
the foot?
A rug.

What is it that goes out black and comes
in white?
A black cow in a snowstorm.

What goes on and on and has an eye in the middle?

Onion.

If athletes get athlete's foot, what do astronauts get?

Missile toe.

What bird lifts the heaviest weights?

The crane.

What is the difference between a home, a sigh and a donkey?

A home is so dear, a sigh is oh dear, and a donkey is you, dear.

What runs into the ground in the morning and doesn't come out until noon?
A plow.

What can you see in winter that you can't see in summer?
Your breath.

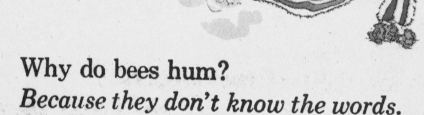

Why do bees hum?
Because they don't know the words.

What trees are left behind after a fire?
Ashes.

If a little lamb is a lambkin, what is a little sleep?
A napkin.

Why is Santa Claus the best gardener in the world?
Because he loves to hoe, hoe, hoe!

What kind of clothing lasts the longest?
Underwear—because it's never worn out.

When is a baseball catcher like a farmer?
When he chases a foul.

What do you find only once in a room, but twice in every corner?
The letter "r."

What is the last word in rockets?
"Fire!"

What bird is always seen in June and July?
A jay (j).

Who are the best bookkeepers?
People who don't return the books they borrow.

What ten-letter word starts with g-a-s?
Automobile.

What is the best way to start a fire with two sticks?
Make sure one of them is a match.

Which of your **parents** is your nearest relative?

Your mother. Your other parent is always father (farther).

What is the difference between a jeweler and a jailer?

One sells watches and the other watches cells.

Why do white sheep eat more than black sheep?

There are more of them!

STATE RIDDLES

What state is a father?
Pa.

What state is a musical note?
La.

What state doesn't feel so good?
Ill.

What state is a number?
Tenn.

What state contains the most metal?
Ore.

What state is a doctor?
Md.

What state is an unmarried woman?
Miss.

What did Delaware to the party?
She wore her New Jersey.

FLOWER RIDDLES

What flower grows between the nose and the chin?
Tulips.

What flower should be kept in a cage?
Tiger lily.

What flower is a great animal?
Dandelion (dandy lion)

What flower do ladies wear on their feet?
Lady's slippers.

What flower comes up with the dawn?
Morning-glory.

What is the first thing a man plants in his garden?
His foot.

Why are flowers lazy?
Because you'll always find them in beds.

NUMBER RIDDLES

Nine ears of corn remained in a farmer's field after the harvesters had gone through it, which was fine for Mr. Rabbit. Every evening, as the moon came up over the barn, the rabbit came and carried away three ears. How many nights did it take the rabbit to get all the corn?

Nine nights. Each time Mr. Rabbit carried away three ears, two of them were his own!

Why is "2 and 2 makes 5" like a left foot?
Because it isn't right.

When do 2 and 2 make more than 4?
When they make 22.

Why is the number 1,000,000,000 bad?
Because it's so naughty.

If a farmer carries a sack of grain and his hired man carries two sacks, which has to carry the heavier load?

The farmer—because the grain is heavier than two sacks.

Seven is an odd number. How can it be made even?

Take away the "s."

A duck behind two ducks, a duck in front of two ducks, and a duck in the middle. How many ducks in all?

Three ducks.

There are four of them in every city and town. What are they?

Letters.

Which is proper to say—3 plus 5 *is* 7, or 3 plus 5 *are* 7?

Neither. 3 plus 5 are 8.

How can you add ten to ten and still have ten?
Put on gloves.

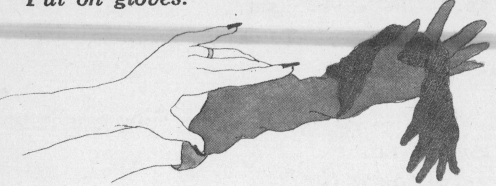

How many two-cent stamps are there in a dozen?
Twelve.

From what five-letter word can you take away two letters and leave one?
Alone.

What number is more when you turn it upside down?
6. (It becomes 9.)

What word of seven letters will have six left after you take away four?
Sixteen.

A man in a butcher shop is six feet tall and wears a size 11 shoe. What does he weigh?
Meat.

BIBLICAL RIDDLES

What fruit kept best in Noah's ark?
The preserved pairs.

Who was the first man mentioned in the Bible?
Chap. 1.

Why was Adam's first day long?
Because there was no Eve.

What is it that may be found in Matthew and Mark, but not in Luke and John?
The letter "a."

Why was the elephant the last animal to get on the ark?
It took him a long time to pack his trunk.

What three words (which read the same backwards and forwards) might Adam have used to introduce himself to Eve?

"Madam, I'm Adam."

When the flood waters went down, was Noah the first one out of the ark?

No, he came fourth (forth).

Where did Noah strike the first nail on the ark?

On the head.

Who is the best doctor mentioned in the Bible?

Job, because he had the most patience (patients).

Where was Solomon's temple?
On the side of his head.

Where is baseball mentioned in the Bible?
The story of creation tells of what happened in the big inning. Another story tells of Rebecca, who went to the well with a pitcher. And another story tells of how Abraham wanted to make a sacrifice.

IN THE AIR

INSTRUCTOR (to student): When you land the plane, we'll taxi down the field.

STUDENT: Oh, that won't be necessary. I have a friend who is picking me up with his own car.

Once there was a man who took a ride in an airplane.

Unfortunately, he fell out of the plane.

Fortunately, he was wearing a parachute.

Unfortunately, the parachute was not properly packed and it did not open.

Fortunately, there was a haystack in the field below.

Unfortunately, there was a sharp pitchfork sticking straight up in the haystack.

Fortunately, the man missed the pitchfork.

Unfortunately, he also missed the haystack.

A man who had never been up in an airplane stopped off at a nearby airport to watch the planes take off and land. With the man was his wife, who had also never experienced the thrill of an airplane ride.

Soon a pilot came by and offered to take the man and his wife for a short ride in his airplane—for $25. It was a tempting offer, indeed, but the man finally decided that the cost was a bit more than he could afford.

"Well, then, I'll tell you what I'll do," said the pilot. "I'll take you and your wife for a ride, and it won't cost you anything, provided that neither one of you makes a sound. If you do make a sound, however, you must pay me the $25."

The offer was promptly accepted by the man, and he and his wife climbed into the plane. The pilot's plan was to get them to cry out. . . and so, no sooner was the plane in the air than he began a series of maneuvers —barrel rolls, loop-the-loops and stalls. But not a sound was heard.

When the pilot eventually returned to the field, he turned around and said, "I must congratulate you, sir, for not uttering a sound during that entire ride. You certainly displayed a good deal of courage by keeping silent."

"Thank you," replied the man. "But I might as well tell you right now, you nearly had me on that deal when my wife fell out!"

ON THE ROAD

POLICEMAN: Anyone who drives as recklessly as you do shouldn't have a driving license.

MOTORIST: That's all right, then. I haven't got one!

X X X

USED CAR DEALER: This is a fine automobile, sir.

CUSTOMER: It looks more like a wreck to me.

USED CAR DEALER: Well, the last owner ran it into a brick wall and the fine was twenty-five dollars.

DOCTOR: Does your hearing bother you when you drive a car?

PATIENT: Yes, it does. Why, I can hear every word my wife says!

Driving along a country road, a lady noticed some repairmen who were rapidly climbing telephone poles. "Will you look at that?" she exclaimed to her companion in the seat beside her. "They must think I've never driven before!"

BOB: Why do you keep such an old car?

BILL: Oh, it's good enough for us—we never go out.

Be careful how you drive! You almost went off the road then.

I thought *you* were driving!

DEE: What model is your car?

LEE: It isn't a model. It's a horrible example!

I notice he always drives around a corner on two wheels.

Yes, that's to save wear on his tires.

31

A lady who was just learning how to drive seemed to be doing quite well. She was at the wheel of the car, her husband was beside her, and the country road did not have too much automobile traffic. But suddenly, the husband was jolted out of his relaxed mood when she screamed, "Quick, Howard—take the wheel! Here comes a brick wall!"

MOTORIST: What's the speed limit around here?

FARMER: There isn't any. You folks can't go through here too fast for us.

A motorist who was driving through a flooded area asked a farmer if it was possible for a car to get through.

"I reckon so," answered the farmer.

Full of confidence, the motorist drove forward. But in no time at all, both he and his car were completely under water.

Sputtering and fuming, the motorist returned to where the farmer was standing. "What made you think that I could drive my car through there?" he shouted angrily.

"Well," answered the farmer calmly, "the water only came up to *here* on the ducks!"

What becomes of all the old cars, Mommy?
Someone sells them to your father.

What are you turning around for?
Oh, I've just found out we've come 510 miles. We'll have to go back to the 500-mile mark and change the oil.

FRANK: What's the difference between this new car and last year's model?
FRED: Well, the cigarette lighter is about an inch closer to the steering wheel.

We've knocked a man down. Aren't you going to stop the car?
Oh, that's all right—we'll read all about it in the papers.

MOTORIST: I haven't paid a cent for repairs on this car since I bought it.
FRIEND: So the mechanic at the garage told me, too.

MECHANIC: Well, I think I've found out why your car won't start. There's a short-circuit in the wiring.
WOMAN: Well, lengthen it, by all means!

Lost on a road in the country, a motorist stopped to ask an old farmer how to get to the city. The farmer then started to give him a long set of directions.

Thirty minutes later, after carefully following the directions the farmer had given him, the motorist found himself once again on the very same road—and there was the farmer, still on the same spot!

"Look!" the motorist shouted angrily. "Your directions brought me right back here!"

"Well-l," drawled the farmer, "I didn't want to waste my time telling you how to get to the city if you couldn't follow simple directions!"

LADY MOTORIST: I'm afraid this accident was largely my own fault.

GENTLEMAN MOTORIST: Nonsense! The blame rests entirely with me. I saw you at least three blocks away and had plenty of time to swerve down a side street.

HOWIE: Does your car always make so much racket?

BOBBIE: No, only when it's running.

WIFE: It's ridiculous for this man to charge us so much for towing our car only three miles.

HUSBAND: That's all right. He's earning it. I have my brakes on!

I see you're allowing your little son to drive the car.

Yes, he's still too young to be trusted as a pedestrian.

POLICEMAN: You were going eighty-five miles an hour on that highway.

WOMAN: Oh, isn't it wonderful? And it's only my first day of driving!

MOTORIST: Do you want a ride to the next town?

HIKER: No, thanks—I'm walking for the exercise.

MOTORIST: Exercise? What's that?

CUSTOMER: Didn't you claim when you sold me this car that you would replace anything that broke?

DEALER: Yes. What is it?

CUSTOMER: Well, I want a new garage door.

ON THE TRACKS

GERT: I have heard that the middle of the train is the safest, so far as accidents are concerned. When there are accidents, the two ends of the train usually get the most damage.

MYRT: Goodness me! Then why don't they take the ends off?

COMMUTER: Your train service is not very good—the cars are always overcrowded.

CONDUCTOR: But you had a seat, didn't you?

COMMUTER: Yes, but my wife had to stand all the way.

ROSS: I commute by train every day. I live in Fishhook.

FLOSS: Fishhook? Where's that?

ROSS: At the end of the line.

BUSINESS MAN: I'd like to catch a late train today.

TICKET AGENT: Take the next train in—that one's always late.

What were your thoughts when you saw the two trains crash head-on?

Well, I thought it was a rotten way to run a railroad.

PASSENGER: Conductor, why is this train running so late?

CONDUCTOR: Well, sir, the train ahead is behind time because of flooded tracks. And the train ahead was behind before, besides.

ON THE SEA

STEWARD (aboard ocean liner): Shall I lay out your clothes, sir? Where are they?

TRAVELER: I put them in that little closet up there with the round hole in it.

STEWARD: I regret to say, sir, that that is the porthole!

A lady on a ship sailing into the seaport city of Athens pointed to some distant white-topped hills and asked a fellow passenger, "What's that over there?"

"I would imagine that that's snow," replied her companion.

"That's just what I thought," said the lady, "but someone else just told me it was Greece."

Nervous Lady (on ocean liner): Do ships like this one sink often?

Captain: No, only once.

Nervous Lady: What would happen if we struck a large iceberg?

Captain: The iceberg would move along as if nothing had happened.

Nervous Lady: Thank you, Captain. I'm so relieved!

Fran: Are you going to England on the "Queen Elizabeth"?

Tran: No, I'm going to Alaska on the contrary.

Passenger: Is there something the matter with the ship, Captain?

Captain: Well, as a matter of fact, the rudder is broken.

Passenger: Well, don't fret about it. It's under water nearly all the time, so no one will notice it.

Why are we on this ship—going to France—when we're supposed to be going to Bermuda?

Well, it's a better ship.

IT'S A PUN, SON

Why is that letter so damp?
Postage due, I guess.

Many gnus had been seen by a hunter during the day. When evening came, his native cook presented him with a delicious steak.

As the hunter finished the steak, he complimented the cook, saying it was one of the best of all possible steaks. As an afterthought, he inquired, "Was it gnu?"

"No," answered the native cook, "but it's just as good as gnu."

WOMAN: Who's in charge of this doughnut factory?
MAN: I am—the hole works.

FREDDIE: My father has a rabbit tattooed on his arm.

TEDDIE: My father has hares all over his chest!

I know a kid with four legs.
How sad!
Crawls about in garbage heaps, looking for food.
How awful!
The parents don't seem to mind at all.
How shocking!
They're goats.

A fisherman once became so tired-out from catching shad that he couldn't row his boat back to shore . . . so he had the shad roe.

You shouldn't go swimming on a full stomach.
I'll swim on my back.

CLARK: What are you doing now?
PARKE: Working on a ranch where they raise hornless goats.
CLARK: But—
PARKE: There are no butts.

Last night I did my homework in one hour.
By the clock?
No, by the television set.

HIRED HAND: I guess I'm a little clumsy at milking this cow.
FARMER: Yes. You have no regard for the feeling of udders.

Mother washed out the picnic jug with a detergent and the liquid was still in there when she answered the telephone. Meanwhile, Father saw it in the jug, thought it was some new kind of drink, and drank it.
Was he mad?
He was frothing at the mouth!

TEACHER: Tommy, what kind of people live in the Po Valley?
TOMMY: Po' people.

Where is the fencing master?
He's out to lunge.

DON: Why do they give girls' names to hurricanes?
DAN: Because they're not "him-icanes."

What shape is a present?

I don't know.

Well, give me one and we'll call it square.

ALAN: I hear that Bruce has bought a coffee plantation.

ADAM: Yes. He's going to learn the business from the grounds up.

Mommy, there's a man at the door with a package marked C.O.D.

Sounds fishy to me!

VAN: Are you taking your horse to Hollywood to appear in movies?

DAN: Yes, he's going to do bit parts.

What do you sell?

Salt.

Why, I'm a salt seller, too!

Shake!

BARRY: I'll have you know that *I* know quite a bit about horses and horsemanship.

LARRY: Well, tell me, what's the broad band that keeps the horse's saddle in place, called?

BARRY: Aw, that's a cinch!

HUSBANDS AND WIVES

HUSBAND: My dear, our household budget is in terrible shape. You've been spending more money than we have.

WIFE: Yes, but that wouldn't have happened if I'd had more money.

VIC: My wife had a funny dream last night. She dreamed she had married a millionaire.

DICK: You're lucky. My wife dreams that in the daytime!

HUSBAND: I have tickets for the theatre.

WIFE: Wonderful! I'll start dressing right away.

HUSBAND: That's a good idea. The tickets are for tomorrow night.

SAL: Is it true about Margie and Harry? I hear that hot words passed between them.

HAL: Yes—she threw a bowl of alphabet soup at him.

DRUGGIST: Well, sir, did that mud pack preparation I suggested improve your wife's appearance?

MAN: It did, for a day or so, but then it wore off.

I broke an expensive dish yesterday.
What did your husband say?
"What hit me?"

MR. MILES: How did that argument you had with your wife turn out?

MR. GILES: Oh, she came crawling to me at last on hands and knees.

MR. MILES: Really? What did she say?

MR. GILES: "Come on out from under that bed, you coward!"

BONNIE: Your husband seems to be a man of rare gifts.

SUE: Oh, he is! He hasn't given me one since we were married!

BRIDE: I have something to confess to you, dear—I can't cook.

GROOM: Well, don't let it worry you. I write poetry for a living. There may not be anything to cook.

JOE: I haven't spoken to my wife in three weeks.

MOE: Why not, for goodness' sake?

JOE: I don't like to interrupt.

I'd rather kiss my wife than eat.

Why? Because she's so attractive?

No—because she's such a bad cook.

So your wife has hay fever. Does it disagree with her?

It wouldn't dare!

Wife's lament: "The way I have to look after that man! Why, whenever he sews on buttons or darns his socks, I always have to thread the needle for him!"

HUSBAND: Aren't you ready yet?

WIFE: I told you an hour ago that I'd be ready in a few minutes!

WIFE: I have a surprise for you. I baked two kinds of biscuits today. Would you like to take your pick?

HUSBAND: It may not be necessary. I'll just use the hammer.

ED: My wife is always asking me for money.

AL: What does she do with it?

ED: I don't know. I never give her any.

MRS. AYE: Tell me, what do you use for washing dishes?

MRS. NYE: Well, I've tried many things, but I find my husband best.

WIFE: Where were you till four o'clock this morning?

HUSBAND: I was sitting up with a sick friend.

WIFE: And what is your friend's name?

HUSBAND: He was too sick to tell me.

How's your wife today?

She can't complain.

Oh, I didn't know she was as sick as all that!

MR. PLINK: My wife is in town—and it's raining.

MR. PLUNK: Well, don't worry. She'll probably go inside some store.

MR. PLINK: That's just what I'm worried about! She'll go shopping!

Agnes just called up to say she couldn't meet you for lunch.

Well, that's a wait off my mind.

WOMAN (on telephone): Hello, Missing Persons Bureau? My husband hasn't been home for two days. I don't know where he could be.

DETECTIVE: Very well, we'll see if we can find him for you. Can you give us a description of him?

WOMAN: Well, he's short, fat, bald, has a grouchy disposition, and dresses like an unmade bed . . . On second thought, just forget about looking for him!

BEN: I'm going to give my wife a washing machine as a Christmas present.

GLENN: I'll bet she'll be surprised, eh?

BEN: You bet! She's expecting a new car.

WIFE: I'm going to give you a piece of my mind.

HUSBAND: Just a small helping, if you please.

BRUCE: Did you ever talk to your wife about saving money?

MARTIN: Yes, I did.

BRUCE: And what happened?

MARTIN: I've got to give up smoking.

COME AND GET IT!

KEN: Have you ever had coconut milk?

BEN: No. Where do you get it?

KEN: Oh, you'd have no trouble finding it. It's the only milk that comes in a hairy bottle.

IMPATIENT DINER: You say you're the same waiter I gave my order to?

WAITER: Why, yes, sir. Why?

IMPATIENT DINER: Somehow I expected a much older man.

DINER: Just give me a ham sandwich.

WAITRESS: With pleasure.

DINER: No, with mustard.

WAITER: Are you through with the finger bowl, sir?

DINER: I haven't even started. I'm waiting for some soap.

DINER: What kind of stew is this?

WAITER: Rabbit stew, sir.

DINER: I thought so. I found some hares in it.

DINER: Just look at this chicken! It's nothing but skin and bones!

WAITER: Yes, sir. Would you like the feathers, too?

All that cake and candy just makes my mouth water.

Here's a blotter.

DINER: I wonder, do you have any cold meat?

WAITER: Well, we have some that's *nearly* cold.

Waiter, I think I'd like some of that blueberry pie.

That's not blueberry pie, sir. Shoo! Shoo!

WAITER: Have you tried the meatballs, sir?

DINER: Yes—and found them guilty.

Do you have any lump sugar?

No, we haven't any lump sugar—only granulated sugar. If you don't like it, you can lump it!

DINER: Please bring me some pins and needles.

WAITER: *Pins?* And *needles?*

DINER: Yes. I'm a sword swallower, but I'm on a strict diet.

JILL: The food in this restaurant is positively poisonous!

BILL: Yes—and such small portions!

DINER: Waiter, this steak is like leather, and the knife is dull.

WAITER: Well, why not strop the knife on the steak?

A man once invited a friend to his home for a rabbit dinner.

When the friend arrived, dinner was ready. It was carrots, peas and lettuce!

DOG DAYS

GUEST (at dinner table): Your dog is certainly very friendly. He keeps looking at me and wagging his tail.

HOST: Oh, I think that's because you've got his dish.

PETE: Come in! Come in!

PAT: I'm afraid to—your dog is barking at me.

PETE: Nonsense! He's wagging his tail.

PAT: Well, I don't know which end to believe.

JERRY: What is your dog—a setter or a pointer?

JOHN: He's neither. He's an upsetter and a disappointer.

Is your dog a good watchdog?

I should say so. If I hear a prowler, all I've got to do is wake him up and he barks.

HOUSEHOLDER: Come right into the yard. Don't mind our dog. Haven't you ever heard the expression, "A barking dog never bites"?

MAILMAN: Yes, but I'm not sure when he's going to stop barking.

HOUSEHOLDER: Nonsense! A dog's bark is always worse than his bite.

MAILMAN: Well, then, for goodness' sake, don't let him bark! He just bit me!

This dog cost only ten dollars, and he's a thoroughbred. That's what I call a bargain!

I should say so—and a bargain dog never bites.

MAN (about to buy dog): Are you sure that this dog is loyal?

OWNER: I'll say! I've sold him five times and he's come back home every time.

HENRY: Is your dog sick? He doesn't look up to scratch.

HENRIETTA: Funny—that's all he does!

THE KIDDY CORNER

BIG GIRL: Do you know how to spell banana?

LITTLE GIRL: Yes, but I don't know when to stop!

MIKE: Have you heard? I have a new baby sister.

IKE: What's her name?

MIKE: I don't know. She won't tell me.

MOTHER: What happened after Jimmy hit you?

TOMMY: He hit me a third time.

MOTHER: You mean he hit you a second time, don't you?

TOMMY: No, I hit *him* the second time.

VISITOR: Well, Emily, tell me—what are you going to do when you grow up to be a big lady like your mommy?

EMILY: Diet, of course.

Mommy, I just found a lost ball.

How do you know it was lost?

The boy across the street is still looking for it.

I hear you've got a new addition at your house—a big, grand baby.

No, you've got it wrong. It's a big baby grand.

RICHARD: I want the wishbone, Mom.

MOTHER: Not until you've eaten your vegetables.

RICHARD: But I want the wishbone, so I can wish I don't *have* to eat them!

Whenever Billy was given permission to share a piece of cake, pie or some fruit with his little brother, Teddy, he always managed to cut or break one piece larger than the other. Naturally, Teddy would always get the smaller portion.

But not any more. Mother made it a rule one day that whenever something was to be divided in half, Billy could still cut it or break it, but Teddy would have first choice of the half he wanted.

Nowadays, things are divided quite evenly, you may be sure!

MINISTER'S WIFE: It was certainly very thoughtful of you, Bobby, to bring over this cake. And I must write your mother a note, thanking her for baking it for our church supper.

BOBBY: Could you thank her for *two* cakes, please?

The cow looked over the fence at the small family group and mooed, loudly and clearly. Then she swished her tail and mooed again.

"Mommy! Mommy!" cried the little boy excitedly. "She blew *both* of her horns!"

SCHOOL DAYS

TEACHER: There will be an eclipse of the moon tonight. Perhaps your parents will let you stay up to watch it.

PUPIL: What channel is it on?

TEACHER: How did this window get broken?

LITTLE BOY: I was cleaning my slingshot and it went off.

TEACHER: Is this wrong? "I have et."
PUPIL: Yes.
TEACHER: What's wrong with it?
PUPIL: You ain't et yet.

TEACHER: Ernest, did your father write this composition?

ERNEST: No—he started it, but Mom had to do it over.

TEACHER: Really, Dexter, your handwriting gets worse every day!

DEXTER: Well, Mrs. Smith, if I wrote any better, you'd just find fault with my spelling

TEACHER: What is the highest form of animal life?

PUPIL: The giraffe.

TEACHER: Dudley, can you tell me what the four seasons are?

DUDLEY: Salt, pepper, mustard and vinegar.

It was raining outside and the kindergarten teacher was helping the children of her class in putting on their raincoats, rainhats and rubbers before sending them home. It was an especially hard struggle with little Billy's galoshes, since they didn't seem to fit too well. She spent more than five minutes getting one of them on Billy's foot and it was almost as long again before the last buckle snapped into place on the second one.

No sooner had she sighed with relief at the job being over, however, than Billy said casually, "You know, Mrs. Betz, these aren't my galoshes."

"They *aren't?*" With a loud groan of helplessness, the patient teacher turned to the task of removing the galoshes. It took just about as long as putting them on.

"Now, then," said the teacher, "whose galoshes *are* these?"

"They're my brother's," replied Billy. "He wore them all of last year, before they got too small for him, and now my mother makes *me* wear them!"

TEACHER: How long did the Hundred Years' War last?

PUPIL: I don't know.

TEACHER: Come, now! How old is a six-year-old boy?

PUPIL: Six years.

TEACHER: Well, then—how long did the Hundred Years' War last?

PUPIL: Six years?

PUPIL: Would you be angry at me for something I didn't do?

TEACHER: Why, I don't see how I could.

PUPIL: Well, I didn't do my homework for today.

TEACHER: If your mother gave you three cookies and asked you to divide them with your brother, what would you do?

PUPIL: Do you mean my big brother or my little one?

TEACHER: Never mind today's date, Tommy. That's not as important as your written examination.

TOMMY: Well, I wanted to have *something* right on my paper.

TALL TALES

One cowboy was bragging to another cowboy about how good a shot he was. "Why," he said, "I can toss a silver dollar high into the air and, taking careful aim, shoot a hole right through the middle of it."

The second cowboy pondered this for a moment, and then said, "Oh, that's nothing! I can stand in front of a mirror and beat myself to the draw!"

A fisherman once caught a fish so big that it took a building crane to lift it out of his boat. He promptly took a picture of it, but he could hardly ever show it to his friends, because it was so inconvenient to carry it with him. The picture itself weighed 20 pounds!

One man was known to have grown so fast in one day that his head was seen to have pushed three inches through the crown of his hat.

There was once a horse that ate so little, and was so thin, it had to wear a blanket constantly to keep the wind from blowing the hay out.

There's no law against talking in Vermont —but there's an understanding no one's to speak unless he's sure he can improve on silence.

Scientists are now working on the development of three-dimensional television. When it is eventually perfected, if you don't turn on the set to see the program, it will come out to see you!

A farmer once had on his farm a rooster that was one of the laziest barnyard creatures that ever lived. Instead of crowing, as it was supposed to do when the sun came up in the morning, it merely waited until some other rooster crowed—and then it nodded its head.

One White Hunter in Africa was glad he had large feet. Once, when he ran out of ammunition, a lion stalked him. He ran as fast as he could, and while he ran, it began to rain quite hard. The lion still followed him. But at last the lion fell into one of the hunter's footprints—and before it could get out, it was drowned.

Buildings are put up very quickly nowadays. One morning a man noticed a construction company digging a foundation for an apartment house and that very evening he saw the landlord putting out tenants for not paying the rent.

A traveler in Florida was attacked by two particularly large and bloodthirsty mosquitoes.

"Come on," said the first mosquito. "Let's take him into the Everglades."

"No, we'd better not," said the other mosquito, who was wiser. "If we do, the other mosquitoes will take him away from us."

In our town, babies are so self-reliant that they walk the floor by themselves at night.

A Texan who was visiting in Australia was asked for his opinion of the ranch on which his Australian host lived.

"Why," said the Texan, "back home in Texas we've got much bigger ranches than this one."

"What do you think of our horses?" the Australian asked.

"Why, we've got much bigger horses than these," bragged the Texan.

Just then a kangaroo hopped by.

"What was that?" asked the Texan.

"What—*that?*" casually remarked the Australian. "That was just one of our pesky little grasshoppers."

Boys grow so quickly in one section of the country that their shadows can't keep up with them.

DUDE: Would you say that good health is the rule out here?

COWBOY: Is it! Why, when they started this place, they had to shoot a couple of men to start a cemetery.

A baseball player once bragged: "I'm fast, all right. When I hit one of my many home runs, I reach first base before the fans even hear the crack of the bat. Once, when I rounded second base, the second baseman said something I didn't like, so I pushed the third baseman in the catcher's lap."

SALESMAN: A man once put a whole bottle of this Miracle Hair Restorer on his bald head. Unfortunately, the hair grew out so fast that he smothered to death before he could lay his hands on a pair of scissors.

A farmer once had a dog so fast that when he ran around the barn, he had to jump over himself every third lap.

Two men who were fond of bragging were passengers on a plane going across the country. The first man complimented himself on his sharp eyesight and the second man never missed a chance to tell about his sharp sense of hearing.

Flying at about 10,000 feet, the first man looked down at the earth and asked his companion, "Do you see that fly walking on the roof of that building down there?"

"No," replied the second man without a moment's hesitation, "but he's certainly making enough noise, isn't he?"

In Kentucky, they breed race horses that are so fast, they cross the winning line ahead of their own shadows.

There are places so rocky in the state of Maine that when farmers plant corn, they look for crevices in the rocks and shoot the grain in with a shotgun.

Once a steam locomotive exploded and the fireman was the only one who escaped, having been blown so far from the place that he was completely out of danger.

Down our way we have a cow that gets hiccups and churns its own butter.

Grand Canyon is quite large. All a man has to do when he goes to bed at night is yell, "Time to get up!" When dawn is breaking, the echo will wake him up.

A man had a bad habit of exaggerating whenever he talked to people. His wife knew about this weakness, of course, and one evening, as the two of them were getting dressed to go to a party, it so happened that the wife had a suggestion to make. "If your stories start getting too tall," she said, "I'll let you know by stepping on your toe. That way, you'll know when to stop."

The husband agreed that this might be a good idea. And with this plan firmly in mind, off they went.

No sooner was dinner over that evening than the man lit a cigar and began telling about a ship he had once seen. "It was 3,000 feet long," he said casually, "500 feet wide, and..."

Just then, his wife stepped hard on his toe.

"... two feet high," he finished weakly.

FUNNY BUSINESS

"I do hope you aren't a clock-watcher," said the employer to the man applying for a job.

"I should say not!" replied the applicant. "I don't like inside work. I'm a whistle-listener."

Boss: Are you looking for work?
Man: Not necessarily, but I'd like a job.

The boss and I had words, and he won't take back what he said.
Really? What did he say?
He said I was fired!

70

BOSS: When I started this business for myself, I had nothing but my intelligence.

EMPLOYEE: My, that was some small beginning!

VOICE ON PHONE: George Smith, your delivery boy, is sick and can't come to work today. He asked that I call you.

EMPLOYER: Thank you very much. Who is this calling?

VOICE: This is my roommate.

EMPLOYER: What do you mean by telling me that you had a college education and six years' experience in a bank when you didn't even get through grade school and never had a job before?

EMPLOYEE: Well, you advertised for a man with imagination!

SALESMAN: I'd like to have a few moments of your time, if I may.

EXECUTIVE: Young man, my time is worth $100 an hour. However, I'll give you ten minutes.

SALESMAN: In that case, sir, if it's all the same with you, I'll take it in cash.

I know a man who wants to hire some help right away. Just take a bath, clean yourself up, and you'll be sure to get a job.

Yes, but suppose I clean myself up and he *doesn't* hire me?

BRASH APPLICANT: Have you an opening for a bright young man?

EMPLOYER: Yes—don't slam it on the way out!

"I'm sorry," said the personnel manager to the young man who stood before him, "but we are overstaffed. We have more employees in our company now than we really need."

"In that case," replied the applicant, "I'm sure the little bit of work I do wouldn't be noticed!"

EMPLOYEE: May I have next Wednesday off, sir?

EMPLOYER: Why?

EMPLOYEE: It's my silver wedding anniversary. My wife's in town and we want to celebrate the occasion.

EMPLOYER: Indeed! And are we going to have to put up with this every 25 years?

As a salesman, I get only two kinds of orders.

What are they?

Get out and stay out.

BOSS: What does this mean? Someone called up and said you were sick and couldn't come to work today.

CLERK: Ha, ha! The joke's on him—he wasn't supposed to call up until tomorrow!

A man walked into his boss's office one morning and demanded a larger salary.

"And just what makes you think you merit a raise in pay?" asked the boss.

"It's only fair," replied the employee. "Everybody is overpaid in this company but me."

EMPLOYER: How long did you work at your last job?

APPLICANT: 65 years.

EMPLOYER: And how old are you?

APPLICANT: 45.

EMPLOYER: How could you work for 65 years when you are only 45 years old?

APPLICANT: I worked overtime a lot.

What happened when you asked your boss for a raise?

He was a perfect lamb—he said "Baa!"

EMPLOYER: I notice from your application that you list your last occupation as cellist. I wasn't aware that you had musical talent.

APPLICANT: Well, I don't exactly—what I mean is, I've just got out of prison

MOE: There are many, many ways of making money in this business.

JOE: Yes, but only one honest way.

MOE: What is that?

JOE: I *thought* you wouldn't know!

BOSS: What's the idea of coming to work almost two hours late?

EMPLOYEE (in bandages): I was in an accident. I was hit by a car.

BOSS: It doesn't take two hours to be hit by a car!

SMITH: I hear that the boss fired you for lying. What did you lie about?

JONES: He fired me for lying about an hour too long in bed every morning.

EMPLOYEE: Sir, I think it's just about time I got a raise. I've worked for the same salary for five years.

EMPLOYER: Well, you ought to be used to it by now.

BOSS: You're fired!

CLERK: May I have the afternoon off to break the news to my wife?

Boss: You're late **again**! Have you ever done anything on time?

Employee: Yes, I've just bought a new car.

The president of a large department store happened to be walking through the packing department one day and there he noticed a young man who was leaning against the wall and whistling.

"How much do you get a week?" the president asked the boy angrily.

"Forty dollars, sir," the young man replied.

Without hesitation, the president of the store took out his billfold, counted four ten-dollar bills, and handed them over to the young man. "There! There's a week's pay!" he snorted. "Now get out of here, you loafer —you're fired!"

Not until later was the president of the store informed that the young man was not an employee of the store—he had merely come by to pick up a package!

Mr. Brown: How long does it take you to get to work?

Mr. Green: About an hour and a half after I get down to the office.

FOREMAN: Do you think you can do hard labor?

APPLICANT: Well, some of the best judges in the country have thought so.

For this job you've got to know French, German, Spanish and Italian. The pay is fifty dollars a week.

Mister, ya got me wrong. I don't know nuttin' like dat. I'm here fer a job in da yards.

Oh, excuse me. See the yard boss. We'll start you in at a hundred and fifty.

BOSS: Do you know what time we begin work at this office, George?

GEORGE: I can't say that I do—they're all hard at it when I arrive.

Are you in business?

Oh, yes, I'm in the sauce business.

How's business?

Worse-dis-year.

EMPLOYER: We can pay you $90 a week now, and $100 a week in six months.

APPLICANT: Thank you. I'll come back in six months.

EMPLOYEE: I put quite a few suggestions for improving the business in the Suggestion Box. Did you receive them?

EMPLOYER: Yes. Did you see the office boy with the wastebasket?

EMPLOYEE: I did, sir.

EMPLOYER: Well, he's carrying out your suggestions.

EMPLOYER: "Flack, you have now been in our employment for twenty-five years. As a token of our appreciation to your length of service and loyalty, you will henceforth be addressed as 'Mr. Flack.'"

How many people work in your office?
Oh, about half.

RECEPTIONIST: Some revenue men were here to see you, Mr. Perkins.

BOSS: What did you tell them?

RECEPTIONIST: I told them you didn't want any.

Do you have any work here?
No, there's no work here.
Then will you give me a job?

WORKER: I must have a raise, sir. I'm in such hardship that I cannot even buy a pair of shoes.

EMPLOYER: Well, I'm afraid we'll just have to let you go. I'm sorry, but bare feet cannot be tolerated at the office.

BOSS: You should have been here at nine o'clock.

EMPLOYEE: Why? What happened?

I hear that Jenkins got a job in a bank. I wonder what it is he does.

Oh, that would be telling.

RECEPTIONIST: A man called a few minutes ago, threatening to thrash you.

BOSS: What did you say to him?

RECEPTIONIST: I told him I was sorry you were not in.

JEAN: I understand you've been studying for months how to increase your salary. Do you think it will be worth while?

JOHN: I don't think so. I just found out today the boss has been studying how to cut down expenses.

SAY "AH!"

PATIENT: Doctor, every bone in my body aches.

DOCTOR: Be grateful you aren't a herring.

DOCTOR: How did you ever get so many scratches and bruises?

PATIENT: It happened in the desert. I swam quite a distance out in a lake before I realized it was a mirage.

DOCTOR: Did you do as I prescribed at the last visit—drink water thirty minutes before going to bed?

PATIENT: I tried to, doctor. I really did. But I was completely full after drinking for only five minutes.

WOMAN: Doctor, I don't know what to do. My son insists on emptying ash trays.

DOCTOR: He's probably merely trying to be helpful. It's nothing very unusual.

WOMAN: Yes—but in his *mouth?*

PATIENT: Well, Doctor, what's my trouble?

DOCTOR: I'm not sure exactly what's wrong with you, but if you were a building, you'd probably be condemned.

Did you recover entirely from the operation?

No, the doctor says I still have two more payments to make.

DOCTOR: That habit of talking to yourself—that's really nothing to worry about, I assure you.

PATIENT: Maybe not—but I'm such a bore!

DOCTOR: Madam, I have just given you a medical examination, and can tell you that all you need is a rest.

WOMAN PATIENT: That can't be true, doctor. I need treatment and medicine. Just look at my tongue.

DOCTOR: That needs a rest, too.

I just had a check-up at my doctor's.
What did he have to say?
He said I was badly run down. He suggested I lay off golf for a while and get a good week's rest at the office.

PATIENT: Why do you whistle while you operate, doctor?

DOCTOR: Well, it helps take my mind off my work.

Doctor, I'm suffering from amnesia.
How long have you had it?
Had what?

PATIENT: How long will it be after I take the anesthetic before I know something?

DOCTOR: Well, now, you mustn't expect too much of the anesthetic.

DOCTOR: If this prescription doesn't cure you, come back and I'll give you something that will.

PATIENT: Couldn't you give it to me now, doctor?

DOCTOR: By the way, may I remind you of that little bill I sent to you last month?

PATIENT: Oh, yes. Well, you told me not to worry about anything.

"Have you done everything I told you to do when you were here last?" the doctor asked his patient.

"All but one," the patient replied. "I'm not able to take that long walk every morning that you suggested. I get too dizzy."

"What do you mean, you get dizzy?" the doctor wanted to know.

"Well, I forgot to tell you," answered the patient. "You see, I'm a lighthouse keeper."

PATIENT: I haven't been feeling very well.
DOCTOR: You look fit as a fiddle, I must say.
PATIENT: Yes, but it takes all of my strength to keep up appearances.

DOCTOR: Those aches and pains in your right arm come with age. They're nothing serious, really.
OLD LADY: Yes—but my left arm is just as old as my right, and I have no pains in it.

PATIENT: Well, doctor, what do you advise?
DOCTOR: You need a good brisk workout twice a day, so instead of walking to and from the railroad station, I advise you to take the bus.

Doctor, remember last year when you suggested that I take up golf to take my mind off my business?

Yes, I remember it very well.

Well, can you prescribe something now to get it back again?

PATIENT: Doctor, I'm a grown man, but I still have a childish fear of thunder. Can you help me to overcome it?

DOCTOR: Why, of course—just do as I do when it thunders—put your head under the pillow and it will go away.

When you are sick in bed, you shouldn't be up and running about.

DOCTOR: Your legs are still swollen, but I'm not worried about it.

PATIENT: Well, doctor, if your legs were swollen, it wouldn't worry me, either.

PATIENT: You're a fraud! I came to you in 1959 for a cold and you charged me $5.

DOCTOR: I cured you, didn't I?

PATIENT: Cured me! Just look at me—I'm sneezing again!

WOMAN: I have such pains in my arms, I can hardly lift them above my head.
DOCTOR: Is that all?
WOMAN: No, it's the same with my legs.

DOCTOR: Are you still taking the cough medicine I gave you?
PATIENT: No. After I tasted it, I decided that I'd rather have the cough.

How much will the operation cost, doctor?
I'll give you cut rates.

PATIENT: Doctor, I'm frightened to death.
This is my first operation.

DOCTOR: I know just how you feel. You're
my first patient.

WIFE: I was at the doctor's today and he
prescribed a change of climate.

HUSBAND: Fine! According to the weather
report, that's just what's coming up tomorrow.

DOCTOR: I'm afraid nothing but an operation will save your life.

PATIENT: And how much will an operation
cost?

DOCTOR: About five hundred dollars.

PATIENT: In that case, let's see what pills
will do.

How are you?

I don't know. One doctor tells me I should
exercise for the good of my kidneys, and another one tells me I should remain quiet for
the sake of my heart.

FARM FUNNIES

FARMER: One of our cows once swallowed a calendar.

VISITOR: Goodness! What happened after that?

FARMER: When we milked 'er, she gave creamed dates.

How's the farm coming?

Fine! Got the fruit stand painted, the refreshment counter open, and the pumps full of gas.

VISITOR: What does your son do?

FARMER: Oh, he's a bootblack in the city.

VISITOR: I see. You make hay while the son shines.

"Shall we take this road back to the city?" the visiting city folks asked from their automobile. They had just helped themselves generously of the fruit of the farmer's many trees.

"You might as well," answered the farmer scornfully. "You've taken almost everything else!"

Why are you running that steam roller over your field?

Well, I figgered I'd raise me some mashed potatoes this year.

FARMER BROWN: I've got a freak at my farm. It's a two-legged calf.

FARMER BLACK: I know it. He was over to call on my daughter last night.

VISITOR: Suppose your farm caught fire. What facilities do you have for putting out the fire?

FARMER: Well, sometimes it rains.

The minister at the country church was just finishing his sermon. "Providence cares for all," he said. "Even the birds of the air are fed each day."

"They sure are!" muttered the farmer under his breath. "Right off my corn!"

HEALTH INSPECTOR: It's not good to have your house built over the pig pen that way.

FARMER: Don't see why not—we ain't lost a pig in ten years or more!

BETH: You mean to say that you live on a farm and don't drink milk at all?

SETH: Nope. We ain't hardly got enough for the hogs.

CITY MAN: I've noticed that you raise hogs here. Do you find that they pay better than, say, potatoes or corn?

FARMER: Not exactly. But you see, feller, hogs don't need hoein'.

FARMER: You're late this mornin', Jed.

HIRED MAN: I reckon I am, but I was kicked by a mule on the way over here.

FARMER: That shouldn't have kept you away a whole hour.

HIRED MAN: Well, it wouldn't have, if he had kicked me in this direction—but he kicked me the other way!

A motorist chugging along slowly on a narrow dirt road saw a farmer and stopped his car to hail him.

"Hello, there," he said. "Do you happen to know if this is the way to West Barleyville?"

"Nope," said the farmer, shaking his head. "Can't say that I know, fer sure."

The motorist started his car again and drove on. About a quarter of a mile later, he heard shouts behind him, and looking, saw the farmer, joined by another man, waving him back. Slowly and carefully he backed his car down the narrow road.

"Well, what is it?" the motorist asked.

"This is my hired hand," said the farmer, indicating the other man. "He don't know the way to West Barleyville, either!"

VISITOR: It must get rather lonesome out here in the country, during the winter.

FARMER: Yep. I don't know what I'd do without my hogs.

CITY BOY: What a nice smooth coat that cow has.

COUNTRY BOY: Yes—it's a Jersey.

CITY BOY: Oh, I thought it was its skin.

There is farm land so poor in some parts of the country that one can't raise a disturbance on it.

VISITOR: Does the wind always blow this way out here?

FARMER: No, it blows this way for half a year and then it turns around and blows the other way.

Did you sell the pigs?

Yes.

What did you get for 'em?

Well, I didn't get as much as I expected to, but I didn't expect to.

FARMER: I thought you said that you had plowed that field.

HIRED HAND: No, I said I was only *thinking* of plowing it.

FARMER: Oh, I see—you turned it over in your mind.

Did you make any money on your tobacco crop this year?

Well, enough to keep me in cigarettes for another year.

That hired hand you once had wants me to give him a job. Is he steady?

Steady? If he was any steadier, he'd be motionless.

What ever became of that man from the city you hired a while ago?

Oh, I had to let him go. He used to be a chauffeur, and he crawled under a mule to see why it didn't go.

The farmer and his niece from the city were watching a cow chewing her cud. "That cow," remarked the farmer proudly, "is one of the best we have."

The girl nodded her head appreciatively. "But," she asked, "doesn't it cost a lot to keep her in chewing gum?"

CITY MAN: Is this bull over here safe?

FARMER: Well, he's a dern sight safer than you are!

One day a farmer and his hired hand discovered a break in the fence going around the pasture. Some hair was found sticking to one of the splintered rails.

"Must have been one of the black heifers that did that," said the farmer sagely.

"Uh-uh—a red heifer," said the hired hand.

"A black heifer," insisted the farmer.

An hour later the hired hand gave the farmer notice that he was quitting. "There's too much argument around here to suit me," he explained.

FARMER: Did you milk the cow?

HIRED HAND: Yes—and I creamed her, too.

COURT SHORTS

PROSECUTOR: Where were you on the night of February 30th, when the theft took place?
PRISONER: There is no February 30th.
PROSECUTOR: Oh, so you stole that, too?

JUDGE: Have you anything to say before sentence is passed on to you?
PRISONER: No, your Honor, except that it takes very little to please me.

JUDGE: Are you guilty of this crime?
MAN: I haven't heard the evidence yet.

Say, have you ever been up before Judge Smith?

I don't know. What time does he get up?

JUDGE: Prisoner, the jury finds you guilty.

PRISONER: That's all right, your Honor. I know you're much too intelligent to be influenced by what they say.

JUDGE: You are accused of shooting squirrels. Have you any plea?

SPORTSMAN: Yes, your Honor—self-defense.

PRISONER: Your Honor, I stole the piano in a moment of weakness.

JUDGE: If that's so, what would you have done if you were strong?

JUDGE: How do you plead to the charge of murder—guilty or not guilty?

PRISONER: That's none of your business!

JUDGE: Ten days—contempt of court!

JUDGE: How can you be so sure you were going only fifteen miles an hour in your car?

MOTORIST: I was on my way to the dentist.

JUDGE: Who was driving when you hit that man?

MAN: No one—we were all in the back seat.

ANIMAL ANTICS

Two sheep were in a meadow.

"Baa-a-a," said one.

"Moo-o-o," said the other.

"'Moo-o-o'?" asked the first sheep in some surprise. "Why do you say 'Moo-o-o'?"

"I'm learning a foreign language," explained the second sheep.

POP KANGAROO: Have you seen our child anywhere, dear?

MOM KANGAROO: Help! Police! I've had my pocket picked.

Why is a snake smart?
You can't pull its leg.

HARRY: My cat was on television once.
LARRY: Really?
HARRY: Yes. Then my mother chased it off so she could dust the set.

As Mr. and Mrs. Leopard finished their Sunday dinner, Mr. Leopard sat back and sighed contentedly. "My dear," he said to his mate, "that hit just the right spots."

Two scavenger goats were poking about among the refuse of a town dump when one of them came upon a can of movie film which had been discarded. Without a moment's delay, he nuzzled open the can and began chewing on the film. Soon it was all eaten up.

"Well, how was it?" the other goat asked.

"Not bad," was the first goat's opinion, "but I think I liked the book better."

LINDA: My, but you have a small cat!

MARGIE: That's because I feed it condensed milk.

The baby sardine swam breathlessly up to his mother. "Come quickly!" he gasped. "There's a big monster close by! I saw it with my own eyes!"

"There, there—calm yourself said the mother sardine soothingly. "Where did you see it?"

"Over there," gestured the baby sardine, flipping his tail.

"Come—show me."

The baby sardine was uneasy about doing it, but with a little more encouragement, he finally led his mother to a spot a short distance away where, sure enough, there *was* a tremendous steel monster rising from the sea bottom. It was a submarine.

The mother sardine glanced at it and giggled.

"Wha-what is it?" the baby sardine asked, all a-tremble.

"My dear, you musn't be frightened by that," laughed the mother sardine. "It's only a can of people!"

That poor elephant has to stand up all the time.

Why?

Well, he gets confused between his trunk and his tail, and can't tell which end to sit on.

Does a giraffe get a sore throat if he gets his feet wet?

Yes, but not until a week later.

SON: Can I give the elephant a peanut, Daddy?

FATHER: Sure—give him two. Business was pretty good this week.

There was once an elephant who thought he was the most magnificent elephant in the whole wide world. In fact, he thought he was the most magnificent elephant who *ever* lived.

The elephant was down by the river one day, getting prettied up before going forth into the jungle. He would dip his trunk into the cool water, then squirt the water high into the air and dash into the falling shower. When he wasn't doing this, he admired his reflection in the water.

As he dipped his trunk into the water for a final rinse-off, an alligator came swimming by and with one quick snap bit off the elephant's trunk!

The elephant glared angrily at the alligator. "Ber-ry fud-dy!" he sneered. "*Ber*-ry fud-dy!"

LADY: Does it cost much to feed this giraffe?

ZOOKEEPER: No. A little goes a long way.

PATTY: Did you know that it takes three sheep to make one sweater?

MATTY: No, I didn't even know they could knit!

A kangaroo hopped into an ice-cream parlor one day, sat down at one of the stools before the counter, and said casually, "Please give me a chocolate ice-cream soda."

"Do you have money to pay for it?" the man behind the counter asked.

"Of course," answered the kangaroo, placing a dollar bill on the counter.

"Very well, then," said the man. He prepared the ice-cream soda, placed it in front of the kangaroo, and took the dollar bill.

"Don't I get back any change?" the kangaroo asked.

"No," the man replied. "Our ice-cream sodas cost exactly one dollar."

As the kangaroo finished the soda, the man said, "You know, we don't see many kangaroos in here."

"I'm not at all surprised," remarked the kangaroo, bouncing toward the door. "And at these prices for ice-cream sodas, you're not going to see any *more* kangaroos!"

HAVE YOU HEARD
ABOUT—?

...The man who was too lazy to walk in his sleep? He hitchhiked.

...The football player who would tackle anything?

...The high-toned family that baited their mousetraps with Camembert cheese?

...The successful tree surgeon who had several branch offices?

...The bumblebee that learned how to play "The Flight of the Trumpet"?

...The mousetrap. It's pretty snappy.

...Miss Muffet's spider? It got in the whey.

... The cowboy who had a seven-horse dinner?

... The dog that visited the flea circus and stole the show?

... The Boy Scout who did so many good turns, he got dizzy?

... The woman who had trouble with her husband and her furnace? Whenever she watched one, the other went out.

... The farmer who fed his cows on birdseed and sold cheep milk?

... The girl who thought foothills were corns?

... The writer who thought and thought, until he got some novel ideas?

... The little dandruff who kept trying to get ahead?

... The contortionist who didn't know where to turn?

JUST ROOMERS

LANDLORD: Do I understand that you have a complaint to make?

TENANT: Yes. The shower isn't working. Would you mind having the hole in the roof shifted over the bathtub?

LANDLADY: How do you like your new quarters?

ROOMER: These aren't quarters. These are eighths!

TENANT: It's raining hard outside and water is coming through the ceiling in several spots. I've told you that this happens when it rains. How long is that going to go on?

SUPERINTENDENT: How should I know? I'm no weather forecaster.

HOTEL GUEST: The room is quite nice, but this wall is too thin. The people in the next room can hear everything I say.

HOTEL MANAGER: Well, to accommodate you, madam, we shall be pleased to hang a heavy tapestry on the wall.

HOTEL GUEST: But then I won't be able to hear what the people next door are saying!

TENANT: When it rained last night, the water came right through the roof and gave me a shower bath. Are you going to do anything about it?

LANDLORD: What do you expect me to do— give you soap and a towel?

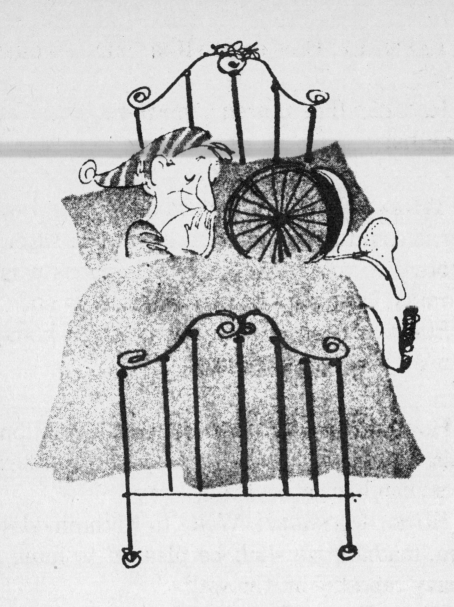

SILLIES

Why did the silly stand in back of the mule?

He thought he would get a kick out of it.

Why did the silly keep his bicycle in his bedroom?

He was tired of walking in his sleep.

What did the silly say when he found nothing on the table for dinner but a beet?
"Well, that beet's all!"

What happened to the silly when he swallowed his spoon?
He couldn't stir.

Why did the silly bring clothes to his lawyer?
Because he had lost a suit.

Why did the silly wear old socks when he played golf?
They had nine holes in them.

If a silly gets up on an elephant, where should he get down?
From a duck.

What song does a silly teakettle like to sing?
"Home on the Range."

Why does a silly think the ocean is friendly?
Because of its waves.

What did the silly call the bird that got caught in his lawnmower?
Shredded tweet.

What did the silly ghost have for breakfast?
Ghost toasties and evaporated milk.

Why did the silly go to the country?
He wanted to see a barn dance.

What did the silly do in the ice-cream parlor with a needle and thread?
Soda cracker.

How does a silly get his clothes clean?
He throws them in the ocean and waits until they are washed ashore.

Why did the silly get up before daylight to do his homework?
If he couldn't get an answer, it would soon dawn on him.

Why did the silly ask his mother to sit on the front steps?
Because he wanted a stepmother.

Why did the silly stop making doughnuts?
Because he got tired of the hole business.

Why did the silly buy chewing gum on the train?
Because he heard the engine saying, "Choo-choo!"

Why did the modest silly go into a closet?
To change his mind.

What did the silly say when he jumped off the cliff?
"This is only a bluff."

Why did the silly laugh up his sleeve?
Because that's where his funnybone was!

What did the silly say when he received a comb as a present?

"Thank you very much. I'll never part with it."

A silly who wanted to reduce sat on a flagpole. Why?

So that his weight would fall off.

Why did the silly in the glass house call for a doctor?

Because he thought he had a window pane.

Why did the silly get his long hair cut?

Because he couldn't stand it any longer.

Why did the silly look for his lost dog in the woods?

Because, by putting his ear close to a tree, he could listen for the bark.

From what dairy did the silly in the Sahara Desert get his milk?

The dromedary.

Why did the silly elephant eat mothballs?

To keep the moths out of his trunk.

Why did the silly name both of his sons
Ed?

*Because he had heard that two Eds are
better than one.*

Why did the silly give a vitamin pill to the
man who had been hit by a car?

*Because he had heard they were good for
rundown people.*

Why did the silly think that the moon was
poor?

*Because he had heard it was down to its
last quarter.*

Why did the silly drink cleaning fluid?

*He wanted to get rid of the spots in front of
his eyes.*

Why didn't the silly rescue his sister when
she fell in the pond?

*Because he couldn't be a brother and assist
'er, too.*

What did the silly say to the ocean, twice
a day?

"Hi, tide!" and " 'Lo, tide!"

What did the silly do when there wasn't enough food to go round?
He served everyone a square meal.

What did the silly call a balanced diet?
Having a piece of cake in each hand.

Why did the silly want to be a bus driver?
So he could tell people where to get off.

Why did the silly forget all about the tooth that the dentist pulled?
Because it went right out of his head.

Why did the silly weigh his watch?
He wanted to see if it was gaining time.

Why did the silly throw all his nails away?
Because the heads were on the wrong end.

Why was the silly able to buy ice at half price?
Because it was melted.

Why wasn't the silly seriously hurt when he fell off the cliff?
Because he had on his light fall overcoat.

MORE SILLIES

A silly walked up to the ticket booth of the movie theatre where a sign read, "Children, 50¢." He pushed a dollar bill toward the cashier and said, "I'll take two, please."

HENNY: Does your cow give milk?
PENNY: No, we have to take it from her.

I just saw something running across the floor with no legs.
Goodness! What was it?
A glass of spilled milk.

SILLY: What are you doing?
BILLY: Knitting a barbed wire fence.
SILLY: What kind of yarn are you using?
BILLY: Steel wool.

For goodness' sake! Bertha is skipping rope. I thought she was sick!

Well, she just took her medicine, but she forgot to shake the bottle.

BONNIE: What are you doing?

RONNIE: Writing to a friend.

BONNIE: But you don't know how to write.

RONNIE: That's all right—he can't read, either.

CLEM: What am I going to do? What am I going to do?

LEM: Why, whatever is the matter?

CLEM: I can't look for my glasses until I find them.

SAM: Where do you work?

TOM: I work at a doughnut factory.

SAM: Really? You have the day off, I suppose?

TOM: No, we're making the holes today.

SWEENEY: What are you looking for?

FEENEY: A quarter.

SWEENEY: Where did you lose it?

FEENEY: I didn't lose it. I just want one.

Why are you constantly scratching your-self?

Nobody else knows where I itch.

NED: What are you doing here?

JED: Nothing.

NED: How will you know when you're through?

NIT: For the sauce you're making, the cookbook says that you must now add a table-spoonful of water.

WIT: Level or heaping?

CUSTOMER: A yard of pork, please.

BUTCHER (to assistant): Give this gentle-man three pigs' feet.

She certainly gets a lot out of a marsh-mallow.

Yes, I noticed that she powdered her nose with it before she ate it.

CUSTOMER: I'd like to buy a pillowcase.

CLERK: Certainly. What size?

CUSTOMER: I don't know exactly, but I wear a size seven hat.

COWBOY CAPERS

FRED: When I was out West, I rode a sure-footed horse.

TED: How do you know he was sure-footed?

FRED: Well, he kicked me in the same place three times!

FIRST COWBOY: So your name is Tex! Are you from Texas?

SECOND COWBOY: No, I'm from Louisiana—but I couldn't stand the fellows calling me Louise!

Who's the oldest settler in the West?
Death Valley Scotty?
Nope.
Buffalo Bill?
Nope.
Daniel Boone?
Nope.
I give up. Who is it?
The sun.

A long day of rounding up cattle on the range and branding them was over. The cowboys had just finished their supper. Two of them were sitting on a bench in front of the ranch house, watching the setting sun.

"Tex," said one of them, "what say we get dressed up and go into town tonight?"

"It sure sounds like a good idea," replied the other cowhand, "but I'd just as soon stay right here. I hear that there's a good eastern on TV tonight."

COWBOY TOM: My horse is very smart. I fell off one day while riding the range . . . and do you know what he did? He galloped into town without being told and brought back a doctor!

COWBOY JOE: You don't say!

COWBOY TOM: Yep. The only trouble was —it was a horse doctor!

The visitor from the city walked up to the cowhands who were sitting atop the corral fence. "What do you fellows use that coil of rope on your saddle for?" he asked.

One of the cowboys answered, "That's for catching steers and broncs."

"How interesting!" exclaimed the visitor. "Do you mind telling me what kind of bait you use?"

COWBOY: Now, if you'll excuse me, little girl, I've got to water my horse.

LITTLE GIRL: What does that mean?

COWBOY: I'm going to give my horse some water to drink.

LITTLE GIRL: Oh, I see. Well, excuse me . . .

COWBOY: Where are you going?

LITTLE GIRL: I'm going to milk my cat.

COMEDY OF ERRORS

A farmer who was passing a lake saw a man in the water a short distance away, floundering about and calling for help. The farmer rowed out in an empty rowboat and soon succeeded in rescuing the man.

"How did you come to fall in?" the farmer asked the man when they were both safely back on land.

"I didn't come to fall in," answered the rescued man. "I really came to fish!"

HOWIE: The last time I saw Cliff, he was mending slowly.

LAURA: Oh, I didn't even know he had been hurt.

HOWIE: He wasn't. He was just sewing up a tear in his coat.

I had it on the tip of my tongue—and now it's gone.

Think hard for a minute. It will probably come back to you.

I doubt it. It was a stamp I was going to put on this envelope, but I think I swallowed it.

MAN (in department store): I'd like some long winter underwear.

CLERK: How long?

MAN: Well, I wasn't thinking of renting it. I wanted to buy it.

"I have found," said the man at the police station, "that the money clip I reported as stolen yesterday was not really lost at all. I'm sorry to have inconvenienced you."

"It's too late now," replied the police chief. "The thief has already been arrested."

TALENTS

MOVING MAN: Pick up that large trunk. Miss Reshoff doesn't want it there.

ASSISTANT: How do you know? Where is Miss Reshoff?

MOVING MAN: She's under the trunk.

He may not be much of a soda clerk, but he's funny.

Yes. He made a banana split yesterday.

A fussy housewife who was having one of the upstairs rooms painted wanted to find out how the painter was getting on in his job, so she listened carefully at the bottom of the stairs. But there wasn't a sound to be heard.

"Are you working?" she called up to the man.

"Yes, ma'am," the painter answered.

"It's just that I couldn't hear you making a sound," she explained.

"Well, after all," the painter said, "I'm not putting the paint on with a hammer."

GEORGE: It took me about six weeks to learn how to ski.

NANCY: And what have you got for your pains?

GEORGE: Liniment.

FATHER: The only way to learn something is to begin at the bottom.

SON: Dad, I want to learn how to swim.

A man approached the owner of a traveling circus and asked for a job. He was told that there was an opening for a lion tamer.

"But I don't know a thing about handling lions," he said.

"It's really quite easy—there's nothing to it," the circus owner assured him. "The whole secret is to force the lions into thinking you're not afraid of them."

The man thought it over for a moment and then came to a decision. "No," he said at last, "I don't think I could be that dishonest!"

Never dive into the water on an empty stomach.

Why not?

The best way to do it is head first.

FIRST HUNTER: You mean to say that you were ten feet from a tiger in the jungle and you didn't shoot?

SECOND HUNTER: Yes. He didn't havé the right kind of expression on his face for a rug.

Where's the astrologer?

He's over at the palmist's, getting his hand read.

Two elderly ladies were discussing the manners of gentlemen.

"George is always very polite on a crowded bus," said one. "When he offers his seat to a lady, he always tips his hat."

"That's true," agreed the other lady. "But Harry does the same thing, yet it's much better."

"How is that?"

"Well, Harry is bigger and heavier than George, you know, and when he gives up his seat, *two* ladies can sit down!"